INTERSECT

INTERSECT

Inspired Personal Reflections

Jane Atkins

To order additional copies of this book, contact:
Xlibris Corporation
1-888-795-4274
www.Xlibris.com
Orders@Xlibris.com
31361

CONTENTS

Dedication

Parents play an integral part in a child's life. As I was growing up, my mother always had words of encouragement, allowing me to experience life. Without this encouragement, I would not have stepped outside my comfort zone to share my passion for poetry with others. In her final struggle with cancer, she was still giving me her support to have my work published. Thus, I would like to dedicate this book to my mother, Edith Mjolsness.

Journaling

Journaling is a form of writing that allows you to express you inner feelings. This expression may help to find the hidden treasures deep within one's mind, or may help to ease pain that we tend to hide inside.

After each poem in this book you will find a reflective thought, helping to guide you in releasing your thoughts on the subjects and themes of the poetry. As you write, allow yourself to open up your inner soul and what may be buried deep inside.

Read the poem, enjoy the words, visualize the possibilities in its relationship to your life.

Try to write as a continuous flowing series of thoughts as the conventions of grammar are not seen by anyone but you.

Do not limit yourself to the number of lines that are on the page as you may find that your journaling will take you within those confines or beyond, depending on the flow from within.

Do not feel bound by the order that the poems are in the book, as the poetry is only an inspiration to help you gain access to what lies beneath.

Most importantly, enjoy life . . . learn from each intersection . . . capture your dreams.

Goals

For many of us it is very important to set goals to work towards in our lives. Goals give us a direction and purpose to the things that we do each day.

We have to be aware that to make goals work for us, they have to be **measurable** and **attainable**. To be **measurable**, one has to be able to see some progress toward the final outcome even if only through very small steps. You must give yourself a quantitative measure of time and/or number so you know when the goal is achieved. To be **attainable**, the goal has to be realistic in its expectations and must always be positively stated. To be **attainable**, a goal can be divided down into many smaller steps that move one in the direction one hopes to go.

Three goals for each person who takes the journey with this book can be stated:

1. **I will choose 5 poems from this book and with the guidance of the reflective thought, I will express my inner feelings through journaling.**
2. **I will read one poem each week and visually reflect, through writing or imagery, on its influence within my life.**
3. **I will complete the journey of inner reflection through poetry by** _____.

(fill in exact date)

Allow your reflections of the influences you have in your life guide you in setting goals for you to reach towards. The future is yours if you capture it. Reach for your dreams.

Intersect

Life is many intersections
we must cross to get ahead,
at times we may need to go straight
but turn right or left instead.

Approaching each intersection
we check for things that we know,
for the people who will help us,
with information we can grow.

Each encounter at a junction
brings us closer to those who care,
thus guiding us gently onward,
with knowledge they choose to share.

We follow the roads we've chosen
to see what our life may hold,
with care at each intersection,
applying all that we're told.

We may sometimes take a wrong turn
as we go along our way.
We may also change direction,
learning more each passing day.

Look forward to each encounter,
learning everything you can,
and at each new intersection,
choose what is best for your plan.

Everyone that you meet and everything that you do creates an intersection in your life.

Each intersection influences where your next step in life takes you. Think back in your life to intersections that have had the most positive influence as to who you are and where you are now. Describe two such intersections and the impact they have had on your life.

_____

_____

_____

_____

_____

_____

_____

_____

_____

_____

_____

_____

_____

_____

Is there an intersection that you would like to occur that would better your future? What steps can you take to guide you towards this intersection?

_____

_____

_____

_____

_____

_____

_____

To Set A Goal

To set a goal
is to have a plan
of things you hope to do.

To set a goal
is to plot the course
and then to follow through.

To set a goal
will create a time
for you to work toward.

To set a goal
will help you
to continue moving forward.

To set a goal
will guide you
and change things that you do.

To set a goal
will help you
try many things so new.

So set these goals
within your life
to help you climb up high.

Set these goals
to reach towards,
don't let your dreams go by.

If we are able to set realistic goals that are measurable and attainable, we will be able to take the positive steps towards changes that may be necessary in our lives.

What would you like to accomplish within a four week period?

Choose one goal to aim towards. List three positive steps that you can take to move towards achieving your goal. Detail how you can tell if you have attained your goal at the end of the four week period.

_____

_____

_____

_____

_____

_____

_____

_____

_____

_____

_____

_____

_____

_____

_____

_____

_____

_____

The Growth of a Mind

A child opens its eyes each morning
anticipating a new day ahead,
wondering what things will happen
once they are out of their bed.
Will there be a fantastic adventure
to share with a very best friend?
Will they be able to travel,
even if it is only pretend?

Thoughts are trapped inside their heads
awaiting stimulation to grow.
Release from the cells will allow
creation with all that they know.
Exploration and challenges presented,
with more advancement each day.
We cherish each new-found idea
while watching a child during play.

With each tiny bit of discovery
learning as no others can,
a movement or a picture can be
part of a very big plan.
What a child can see of the future
is something we truly can't say,
but we know that experiences
help them, develop more
with each passing day.

We all have a challenge to look back at where we have come from.

What impact did incidences from your childhood have on the person you are today? Describe two incidences from your childhood that have been a positive growing experience, helping you step up to your life today.

_____

_____

_____

_____

_____

_____

What one dream did you have as a child that you are still trying to achieve today?

Set a goal that you can achieve within four weeks that will move you closer to fulfilling this dream.

_____

_____

_____

_____

_____

_____

_____

_____

_____

Did you . . .

Did you see that?
What I ask?
. . . that tiny spider on the glass.

Looking hard I hoped to see
Something there in front of me.

Did you see that?
Where I ask?
. . . way up there, the clouds will pass.

Looking hard, the sky soon cleared,
and an angel soon appeared.

Did you hear that?
What I ask?
. . . that rustling sound from yonder tree.

Listening hard I hoped to hear,
a bird's chirping drawing near.

Did you hear that?
Where I ask?
. . . something close to you and me.

Listening hard I hoped to hear,
something of which I had no fear.

Did you know that?
What I ask?
. . . that life is learned from all around.

Answering quickly, yes, I know,
what we see and hear helps our minds grow.

My granddaughter is always questioning happenings around us. It made me aware that we sometimes don't see the simple things around us that may unknowingly change our lives. We don't hear the pleasant, calming sounds of life, only the steady drone of progress. Take time tomorrow to look around you . . . take time to listen to the gentle sounds.

How have the new sights and sounds you have experienced in the past 24 hours influenced your well-being and your outlook on another tomorrow?

_____
_____
_____
_____
_____
_____
_____
_____
_____
_____
_____
_____
_____
_____
_____
_____

The Cowboy Poet

I sat down at my desk
with my trusty pen in hand,
pondering words to write
about this expansive land.

The words flowed out quickly
about things that I knew,
the ideas soon expanded,
some wild but some true.

I included some humor
for laughter is good.
It makes people feel
the way that they should.

I wrote a whole story
of how the west was won,
I enjoyed all my writing
its my way to have fun.

My imagination soared
to heights was above,
I poured out my feelings
of things that I love.

One cannot stop writing
the tales of the west.
I just hope that I'm better
than all of the rest.

Laughter is an essential ingredient in everyone's life. The cowboy poet takes events and gives them a humorous twist, along with putting a little of themselves into their work.

When was the last time you laughed over something that you read? How can you take any situation in life and find the humor in it to lighten the load?

Express your thoughts about three incidents you have found humorous in the past six months, noting how each made you feel at the time.

_____

_____

_____

_____

_____

_____

_____

_____

_____

_____

_____

_____

_____

_____

_____

_____

_____

Linear View

Life is a set course,
straight as the eye can see.
There should be deviations,
I'm sure you'll all agree.

If there were no curves thrown at us,
our minds would slowly cease,
by following the straight and narrow,
would your life still be a breeze?

We need challenges in our lives
to keep an active mind,
creating new paths to follow,
new memories to find.

Let not your life be stagnant,
excite your mind anew.
Step off the narrow pathway
to let ideas through.

Abandon linear thinking,
hidden within your brain,
allowing your mind to wander . . .
excite your life again.

Life can be very boring if one allows their life to become robotic. You must deviate from the monotonous cyclical nature of life to grab new experiences and to advance your mind and soul.

Think of two deviations you have taken within in last month that have changed your life in some little way. Express how these changes has been a positive influence in your life.

_____
_____
_____
_____
_____
_____
_____
_____
_____
_____
_____
_____
_____
_____
_____
_____

This week reflect on deviations you could take to step out from your linear view. Write three steps that you can take to move towards a new experience that will add to your life.

_____
_____
_____
_____
_____
_____

Nature's Call

Upon the mountains I will look
in spring and then in fall,
as if a picture in a book
awaiting nature's call.

As I watch the flowers grow,
a quiet peace inside,
deep feelings then begin to flow
with nature I abide.

As the birds begin to sing,
I listen to their songs.
The happiness that this will bring
makes one forget all wrongs.

A zephyr stirs nature to move
the seeds and leaves and trees,
as if to aver and to prove
the strength of a gentle breeze.

Hearken now, a babbling brook
is calling to us all.
There is no picture in a book
to mimic nature's call.

Take a look at nature around you. Listen to its sounds and see its beauty. What influence can nature have on your life? What do you find most calming? What do you find most annoying? What two ways can nature call you to ease your mind on a stressful day?

_____

_____

_____

_____

_____

_____

_____

_____

_____

_____

_____

_____

_____

_____

_____

_____

_____

_____

At Day's End

Now the day comes to an end
and the sun is setting low,
creating vibrant colors,
allowing a calming glow.

This is a time to reflect
on some things that have now passed,
and to store within our hearts
fond memories we hope last.

As the colors gently change,
each one a brilliant hue,
we think of each day's passing
and the peace of life anew.

Let the colors of the sunsets
create calm each passing day,
in all life's trials or pleasures,
whether found in work or play.

Take time to view the sunsets
seen westward each passing night,
to free yourself of burdens
and to let your dreams take flight.

As the sun sets, take time to watch the gradual fading of the colors. Reflect on what has influenced your life in a positive way in the past two weeks. How can you use this knowledge to increase your successes in the future? Set two goals that will step you closer to increasing your successes whether at home or at work within the next two weeks.

_____

_____

_____

_____

_____

_____

_____

_____

_____

_____

_____

_____

_____

_____

_____

_____

_____

_____

Like a Rock

Obstacles are ever present
in the daily course of life,
like a rock within a harbor,
each one causing someone strife.

You have to choose the side to take
to solve the problem at hand,
unlike a rock in a harbor,
there are things to understand.

You must question things that happen
to make sure your path is clear,
going around some obstacles,
troubles soon may disappear.

Like a rock within a harbor,
there may be a guiding light,
to indicate the path to take,
keeping trouble out of sight.

The waters may be rough you know,
whichever path you may choose,
unlike a rock within a harbor
you can win or you can lose.

Everyone has obstacles to overcome as they journey through life. It doesn't matter if you are rich or poor, you will still stumble at times. What has been your main obstacle as you move through life? What guidance have you received to find a way around the obstacle, to put it behind you?

Can you see an obstacle in your near future? What steps can you take to move around this obstacle smoothly? What will you do if this obstacle is more difficult to maneuver around than you anticipated?

_____

_____

_____

_____

_____

_____

_____

_____

_____

_____

_____

_____

_____

_____

_____

_____

_____

_____

Time

Time . . .
moving swiftly . . .
A bullet . . .
gone . . .
not to be captured.
Only a memory remains
of what once was.

Remember
the past . . .
A mirror
reflecting . . .
clearing one's mind,
understanding
things gone.

Wonder
your future . . .
A lantern
leading the way.
Guiding you onward,
lighting your way.

Take time . . .
reflect . . .
remember . . .
learn . . .
proceed.
Let time guide you
in your search
for where
you hope to be.

Time is only one element that affects our lives. We are continually surrounded by the need for time whether it be the time for work, the time for family, or the time for leisure. It can mean you are either late or early, slow or fast. How does time dictate your schedule? What aspect of time affects your life the most? In what way can your reliance on time have a positive influence on your future?

_____

_____

_____

_____

_____

_____

_____

_____

_____

_____

_____

_____

_____

_____

_____

_____

_____

_____

Sunset Serenity

Peace within,
calming thoughts
as colors permeate the sky . . .
the sun setting
to end another day.

Tranquility felt,
serenity spreading
as the hues gradually fade . . .
ending the trials
presented this day.

Quiet your mind,
inner harmony
as the colors meld . . .
giving us a stillness
to reflect upon
our day.

Look at sunsets and feel the calming effect they have as you drink in the ever-changing colors and hues. A sunset is the end of a day, but in reality it is also the beginning. It commences your rejuvenation for the day to come. It is the start of new thoughts about what lies ahead as one reflects upon what has passed. Ponder the new beginnings you have before you and a sunrise, as beautiful as a sunset, can give you the energy to spring forth.

What new beginning would you like to make? What three steps do you have to accomplish to move towards this new beginning? How soon would you like this to happen?

_____

_____

_____

_____

_____

_____

_____

_____

_____

_____

_____

_____

_____

_____

_____

_____

_____

Success

Success is not seen . . .
It is understood . . .
by your actions with and towards others.

It is present . . .
even for the smallest accomplishment.

It penetrates . . .
obstacles placed in your path.

It emits . . .
an aura of well being in you.

It is ever present . . .
with your positive attitude.

It flows . . .
as your thoughts progress.

Success is within you.

Reflect within, to your own successes.
Make a list of seven of your successes in life.
What allowed you to be successful in each incident?
What success is within you this year?
Write about the steps that you can take to achieve this success.

_____

_____

_____

_____

_____

_____

_____

_____

_____

_____

_____

_____

_____

_____

_____

_____

_____

_____

_____

What a Child Can Teach

A child is a teacher
to all those around.
Each adventure they go on
there is learning found.

They teach us to cherish
each lesson so small.
They teach that on Earth
there is room for all.

We learn that the truth
is the best to express.
We learn that it is best
not to try to impress.

Instruction is given
about showing we care.
Instruction is followed
in ways we can share.

Watch as a child
experiences each day.
And see what we're taught
as they work and play.

Let these lessons guide you
although from a child's mind,
as they will help us remember
what we've left behind.

We, as children were teachers to all around us. We didn't know that people cherished our laughter and the joy we expressed with each new experience. Reflect on two experiences you have had where a child has been the influence of your actions or thoughts. What positive effect has a child had on your life?

_____

_____

_____

_____

_____

_____

_____

_____

_____

_____

_____

_____

_____

_____

_____

_____

_____

Ribbons

Each stream of our life
is as a ribbon floating;
wafting gently with the breeze,
falling softly to the earth . . .
crisscrossing all the ribbons
that have fallen before.

Each strand of our life is a ribbon. It begins and continues on until we choose to cut it free. Even once cut, these ribbons have affected all aspects of our life to that point. Some ribbons crisscross, changing our course of life.

Reflect when two or more ribbons for your life intersected to alter your course. Describe how each ribbon influenced positive changes in your life's journey.

_____

_____

_____

_____

_____

_____

_____

_____

_____

_____

_____

_____

_____

_____

_____

_____

_____

Eye of the Cave

Each day we discover the wonders of Earth,
the beauty that is present
in all that surrounds us,
yet, beneath us are hidden
treasures untold.

Caverns spread forth magically
as nature creates mystic realms
unseen by those above.
Yet, upon discovery,
the mystery will unfold.

The darkness below
is as a lost soul
until the light filters from the surface
to illuminate and present
an awe-inspiring scene.

The colors so pure and untouched
by the devastation
seen in the world above,
a place truly tranquil and serene.

The undisturbed miracle of nature
creating a deeper understanding of life,
inner peace and harmony within reach.

The eye of the cave,
an ever-changing portal,
reflecting new light into our minds and souls,
guiding our thoughts
to those we teach.

Absorb the beauteous scene surrounding,
to learn more of the structure of life,
clearing one's mind of everyday strife.

What natural beauties create calm in your life? Look beyond the four walls that surround you to find nature's simplest gifts. Which treasures of nature allow you inner peace?

Take time to surround yourself with nature and describe the de-stressing characteristics your encounter, that you can then rely on the make your life better.

_____

_____

_____

_____

_____

_____

_____

_____

_____

_____

_____

_____

_____

_____

_____

_____

_____

_____

Union

Under the spreading palms,
protected from the sun,
the red carpet lay
strewn with aromatic petals,
awaiting a special union.

Behind, one hears
the lapping of the waters
on the pure white sand,
urging the procession onward,
the ever present breeze
whispering to commence.

Then, beaming from above,
a spotlight from the heavens,
giving consent
as two become one.

Weddings are very special no matter the location of the ceremony. Surrounding oneself with family and friends helps to add to the feeling of unity. When a union is witnessed by people who have intersected your life, they too become part of the union, part of the new sphere of influence in your life. A marriage is only one time of union within ones life. Describe two unions you have had within your life, and the sphere of influence that has accompanied these special happenings. How have the people continued to be a part of your life?

_____

_____

_____

_____

_____

_____

_____

_____

_____

_____

_____

_____

_____

_____

_____

_____

_____

_____

Aftermath

Yes, I'm bald and have no hair,
as many people laugh or stare.
The feelings hidden deep inside,
help me to shed the words some chide.
Times have been trying as you know,
but as I get better hair will grow.
The chemicals used to kill the cells,
cause many problems, no one tells.
So many things I must endure,
as for cancer there is no cure.
Remission is now my utmost goal,
but all the treatments have taken their toll.
To be healthy again is what I'd like to be,
and from this disease I'd like to be free.

Do you know anyone in your circle of influence who has endured a life threatening illness? What effect did their challenges have on you? Reflecting back, what could you have done differently to ease the situation, or change the outcome? What do you do within your life to help others cope with unexpected illness?

_____

_____

_____

_____

_____

_____

_____

_____

_____

_____

_____

_____

_____

_____

_____

_____

_____

_____

Sense Life

Adventure life . . .

Step outside your protective zone.
See the world
from a new perspective.

Hear sounds
that will bring calm to your life.

Smell the natural world
that surrounds you.

Taste the fruits
of your labors of love.

Touch the hearts
of those you encounter.

Feel the love
you emit from your heart.

Cherish the memories
you will make.

Reflect on this
new life adventure.

If we don't step out of our protective realm, we become more and more sheltered. To progress forward we need to use all of our senses. What effect has each of your senses of touching, tasting, hearing, seeing, or smelling had on your life in the past week. Choose one sense to track for the next week and journal the influence that it has had on your life.

_____

_____

_____

_____

_____

_____

_____

_____

_____

_____

_____

_____

_____

_____

_____

_____

_____

Intertwined

Lives are a never-ending entanglement
of people we meet each day.
Whether or not we know it,
the affect us in so many a subtle way.

Many things shape the lives we live each day,
dictating to us how we feel,
even the animals we surround ourselves with
give us a deep love so real.

Each day as we tend to the animal's needs,
their actions and emotions we see.
The attachments grow stronger each passing day,
I'm sure that you all will agree.

Then, in an instant, the bond can be snapped,
striking something so deep inside,
to have cared for them, nurtured them, shared in their lives,
then to take their departure in stride.

Our love remains strong, though we ask ourselves
why we have to endure all the pain,
why we are tested each day of our lives,
its something no one can explain.

One thing that we learn throughout these ordeals
is that the entwining is strong.
We rely on each strand that is gradually built
hoping its strength will last long.

As each connection is made throughout our lives
it allows us to inwardly grow.
To expand our hearts, our minds and our souls
to remember all we now know.

We will never understand the trials of life
but the entangled web that we weave
will always support us and give us our strength
as ones dear to us sometimes may leave.

Whether it be a personal or natural bond,
the strength of it is all from inside;
hold the connection, cherish memories and times
and take each new day in stride.

As life throw us new challenges each day,
follow your heart to the strand
of the entangled web in your life
that will allow your to understand.

Each person we meet, in all aspects of our lives, has an influence on who we are, what we are doing, and where we are going. Think back through life to three people who have had a positive influence on you, no matter how small. How did each of these people change your direction? Presently, who is intertwined in your life, creating a positive relationship, affecting your feelings or decisions?

_____

_____

_____

_____

_____

_____

_____

_____

_____

_____

_____

_____

_____

_____

_____

_____

Lifting the Fog

We arise to a new day,
unclear of what life will bring,
or the steps we need to follow.

Life a ship enshrouded,
we too are searching for
where we want to go.

Gradually the fog begins to lift
and we see the light
that will guide us.

At yet . . .
another day dawns,
again there is a haze.

Now we know to set goals,
to focus our minds,
removing the murkiness.

We guide our ships,
our minds and bodies,
with clarity in our lives.

Reflect on the uncertainties that you face each day. What has allowed you to create the clarity with these uncertainties? Who or what has influenced you to shed light on your murky moments?

_____

_____

_____

_____

_____

_____

_____

_____

_____

_____

_____

_____

_____

_____

_____

_____

_____

A Less Traveled Road

As we look out across the landscape,
placed by nature for us to view,
we contemplate the peace and solace,
creating inward feelings new.

The sky a swirl of soothing colors,
gently calming our fears and stress,
the leaves upon the trees now ablaze
with colors to relieve distress.

We are drawn magically to the
mountain scene, in the east or west,
hoping for a special place for us
to unwind our lives, and then to rest.

To let nature fully surround us,
to seep into our hearts and souls,
to relieve the pressure created
from reaching for life's changing goals.

This narrow road is one less traveled
due to the hectic pace of life.
We do not take the time to correct
what has caused all of our strife.

Follow the road less traveled today
as nature may change you, you know.
Allow the calm to settle within,
your new peace will outwardly show.

You will then be able to confront
new challenges you face each day,
and return once more to nature
with changes in your life to stay.

Return on the road less traveled now,
each day you require the time,
reflecting upon the trials of life,
creating a new life sublime.

Getting away, even if only to a small cabin in the woods, helps to give a calming, to clear one's mind. What would be your ultimate get away that would allow you to create calm in your otherwise busy life? What steps can you take to achieve this time to cleanse your inner soul?

_____

_____

_____

_____

_____

_____

_____

_____

_____

_____

_____

_____

_____

_____

_____

_____

_____

Rain

Droplets are forming
on the window pane,
causing one to reflect
on life once again.
The calming beating
of this silent drum,
splashes that bounce up
one by one,
rhythmically leading
one's mind astray,
inwardly seeking
to find a way
to keep one's life
moving smoothly on
and hoping troubles
are quickly gone.
The droplets slowly
begin to run,
soon our reflections
will be done.

Watch as the rain travels down a windowpane, and the many paths it takes to reach its final destination. It is as in life, as we tend to take the easiest path to reach a chosen destination. Reflect on one simple path you took. Evaluate what may have happened if you had randomly chosen other directions on your journey to you final destination.

_____
_____
_____
_____
_____
_____
_____
_____
_____
_____
_____
_____
_____
_____
_____
_____
_____
_____
_____
_____

Choices

Look around,
find something new,
choosing correctly,
understanding what's true.

Make things happen
to better your plan,
keep your life on track,
a hurdle to span.

Correct your wrongs,
making them right,
doing things calmly,
don't make it a fight.

Take each step slowly,
making it count,
carefully avoiding
troubles that mount.

Look forward in life
to where you will be
as each step you take
will help you be free.

We tend to take steps in many directions throughout our lives. Sometimes we may not take a step that moves us forward, but it is still a choice of a direction that we see our lives taking at that point in time. Look around you as you progress through each day. Choose something new that you want to accomplish and describe the steps you need to fulfill this step in your life's plan. Be sure to acknowledge when each step is complete and if the next step is moving you forward.

_____

_____

_____

_____

_____

_____

_____

_____

_____

_____

_____

_____

_____

_____

_____

_____

_____

Influences

What causes you to do
the things in life each day?
What choices have you made
in your work and in your play?

Have your decisions always made
your life pass by with ease?
Have you thought through all your actions
so they go by like a breeze?

Can you think of what is best
for you and the ones you love?
Can you hope for things to happen
with the help from those above?

When can your motives to succeed
help others you may know?
When can your experiences build
confidence to help you grow?

How can each thing you do each day
influence the world around you?
How can the dreams you strive for
relate to friendships found?

Let these questions now
be ever-present in your mind.
as influences that you will have
will better all mankind.

Although you may not realize it, you are a big influence to all those around you; from the giving of a simple gift, to sharing your thoughts with others. Each day in the next week, write one way in which you have influenced someone else's life. Note how your influence was important to you.

_____

_____

_____

_____

_____

_____

_____

_____

_____

_____

_____

_____

_____

_____

_____

_____

No One Ever Told Me

No one ever told me why birds soar so high,
and I never asked why not all of them fly.

No one ever told me why thoughts come from above,
and I never asked about the many hurts of love.

No one ever told me why cancer can take a life,
and I never asked why in this world there is such strife.

No one ever told me how to raise a child
and I never asked what makes them meek and mild.

No one ever told me about how to show I care,
and I never asked what feeling I had to share.

I wish I had the answers now,
but in my mind I question how.

We are constantly asking questions to understand life around us. We do not know all of the answers and so many times we are afraid to ask as it may make us seem unknowledgeable. Yet, to understand where we are going, we have to question each step we take to make sure we keep on track. For the next week, write the questions that have been most pressing to you and jot down where the answers were, or could have been found.

_____

_____

_____

_____

_____

_____

_____

_____

_____

_____

_____

_____

_____

_____

_____

_____

Inside My Head

I have many secrets
deep inside my head.
Many, many secrets,
some cannot be said.
Reflecting on these secrets
can change my frame of mind,
hoping for some answers,
nothing soon to find.
As I talk to others,
I find I'm not alone.
Some of my deep worries
have grown wings and flown.
Never more to bother
deep inside my head,
I'll fill the void with knowledge
I enjoy instead.

We all have parts of our lives we may choose to hide. There are parts of these memories that come forth, with glimpses of our past. We need not bury them forever. Talk about solutions or changes these memories have made to your life. Some secrets that we share, may help others find answers, or even create answers to our own situations. Bring forth a secret you need to share and discuss how sharing it could help your resolution and possibly also help others.

_____

_____

_____

_____

_____

_____

_____

_____

_____

_____

_____

_____

_____

_____

_____

Line ups

The school bell rings
a rush to the door,
forming a line,
but, what else can one do?

The cart loaded high
with necessities of life
a long line to pay,
but, what else can one do?

The bride and groom smile
greeting each as they pass
a family line created,
but, what else can one do?

Children's joy echoes
anticipating the fun
the ride line lengthening,
but, what else can one do?

Security is essential
as we soar through the sky
screening lines growing,
but, what else can one do?

The conference begins
registration a must
making friends in the lines,
but . . . .
what else can one do?

Everywhere we go in today's society we have a line to wait in. We cannot avoid them, as they seem to have become a necessity of life. At a recent conference, it seemed that there was a line for everything, everywhere we went. But, something good came out of these lines. The lines gave many of us time to talk and share a part of us. A lot of times, the people that we met in the lines became our friends. Think back through your life to a time where you met someone who became part of your life due to the two of you being at the same place, at the same time. Explain how the relationship grew, and where that relationship is today.

_____

_____

_____

_____

_____

_____

_____

_____

_____

_____

_____

_____

_____

_____

_____

_____

Surround

Surround yourself with color,
let the light shine brightly through,
blending smoothly together,
to create that something new.

Take a blue from way up high
and indigo from below . . .
Mixing thoughts that we may have,
helping our minds grow.

Yellow brightly beaming down,
enlightening treasures found,
an orange glow then smothers
new images all around.

At times we may see red
when things don't go our way.
Yet, with some effort on our part
violet permeates the day.

Look towards the pot of gold
that some hope that they will find,
at the end of the great rainbow
created in one's mind.

Surround yourself with colors that stimulate your inner feelings. Calm your mind as the colors merge. What color is the most significant in your life? Why is it important to you?

_____
_____
_____
_____
_____
_____

Do any other colors hold any value to your life? What effect do they have?

_____
_____
_____
_____
_____
_____
_____
_____

Giving

When we are pushed beyond our bounds,
something deep within we hear . . .
outwardly putting on a brave face,
inwardly cowering in fear.

There is an unknown fear around us
that we encounter each day we live,
with natural and man-made disasters
each person hoping for the other to give.

With an out-stretched hand we must consider
which way our help is the best,
can we physically give of ourselves
or a pay off just like the rest?

Money is only material, yet helps
to pay for things to be done,
but the help that one gives
must come from the heart
to be considered as number one.

We all have had the opportunity to give to charitable organizations to help others. We all do so in our own way. When was the last time you gave either physically or monetarily to a cause? How did this make you feel? What were the consequences of your giving within yourself, and within those to whom you gave?

_____

_____

_____

_____

_____

_____

_____

_____

_____

_____

_____

_____

_____

_____

_____

_____

_____

Fortune

Look around you at the fortunes
that you now possess,
treasures that you have amassed
while trying to impress.

Bat all the fortunes cannot be seen
as they are not all viewed through sight,
the friendships made throughout one's life
are held deep in one's heart . . . tight.

Our friends empower us to do
what is within our heart,
each a gentle persuasion
helping us to make a start.

The unknowingly guide us
through the trials of life each day,
by showing that they care about
things we do and say.

The bounty of a friendship
is a filled treasure chest,
and a true friend is a fortune
better than the rest.

Have you had a true friend at sometime in your life that you could consider a true fortune? Are they still a part of your treasure chest? Have you let them know how important they are to your life?

_____

_____

_____

_____

_____

_____

_____

_____

_____

_____

_____

_____

_____

_____

_____

_____

_____

_____

_____

Changes

As autumn settles in,
changes take place.
Leaves change color and fall
as if full of grace.

The colors begin
to swirl to the ground,
settling here and there,
beauty all around.

Yet, this is not
seen as being the end,
it is another beginning
of a new life, my friend.

New seeds in the ground
will be planted deep,
with the snows of winter,
the moisture to keep.

Then in spring
a new shoot will sprout,
and about this new life
we'll sing and we'll shout.

Praise to the earth
from which new life springs,
rejoice in the flowers
and most natural things.

Each passing day we see changes and growth all around us. What changes have you witnessed in the past year, that have caused you to grow as a person?

_____

_____

_____

_____

_____

_____

_____

_____

_____

_____

_____

_____

_____

_____

_____

_____

_____

A Child's Imagination

A child's Imagination
is a place for them to hide,
away from all the troubles
that may be deep inside.

They may go on an adventure
to places near and far,
challenging unknown rebels
or becoming a shining star.

A wondrous world around them
with something new at every turn.
Oh, to be a child again,
is something we all yearn!

Childhood is usually a carefree time of learning and living free. It is a time when we begin building our futures through our dreams. If you were a child again, what would be within your realm of imagination? What would be your escape? What would your dreams be?

_____

_____

_____

_____

_____

_____

_____

_____

_____

_____

_____

_____

_____

_____

_____

_____

_____

_____

Reflect Within

Look inwardly to understand
where you want your life to go.
Reflect upon what makes you tick,
understanding all you know.

As if within a well lit cave,
with water all around,
your mind is harbored deep within,
hidden memories soon found.

Look deep within the cavern walls,
for hidden from common view
are secrets once buried from all,
revealed to only a few.

Let the calming of the waters
open your inquiring mind,
probing deep inside your memory,
many a treasure to find.

Although outside influences can alter where we go in life, there is an inward influence that should be strong. Within your mind are memories that are the stepping stones as to who your are and where you have gone. What three things can you reflect upon that will help you to your future goals? What three things do you wish to accomplish this month and what past stepping stones may help you to achieve these?

_____

_____

_____

_____

_____

_____

_____

_____

_____

_____

_____

_____

_____

_____

_____

_____

_____

_____

Wind

The howling sound I dread to hear
is the north wind soon drawing near.
A zephyr first begins to blow,
next a strong gale, as we well know.
It picks up things here and there
taking them swirling through the air.
Dropping them silently as it moves,
depositing drifting dirt in grooves.

The fine black soil that was found on top
is now a part of the neighbor's crop.
Tie down your hat or it may fly
off your head and into the sky.
Trees and buildings or anything tall
wave back and forth as if they might fall.
Lake water laps against the shore
beating the sand dunes more and more.

If this great power we could contain,
what could we do, now let me explain;
use of this energy would let us
operate more things without a fuss.
We'd keep its strength for another day
when clouds in the sky aren't quite so gray.
The winding path the wind will soon choose,
let us capture it now for all to use.

Wind as a sustainable energy form is emerging. It is not the only form of energy that affects us. What sources of energy are present in your life? How can you use these energy sources to make your life run more smoothly? In the future, what energy source do you feel will be the most universal?

_____

_____

_____

_____

_____

_____

_____

_____

_____

_____

_____

_____

_____

_____

_____

_____

Gone

I saw you suffering
but what could I do?
I saw your tears as
your pain was so true.

I heard your pleas,
what could I give?
I heard your cries as
you wanted to live.

I watched your struggles
with each passing day.
I watched as this cancer
took you away.

I saw you at peace
as you rested your head.
I saw your life pass
to God's hands instead.

I remember the strength
that you gave to me.
I remember the moment
your spirit was free.

I stayed at my mother's bedside as cancer slowly consumed her body. I tried to help her ease the pain. Throughout the ordeal, although she was the one suffering, it gave me strength to face the trials I have in life. How has the passing of another given you strength?

_____

_____

_____

_____

_____

_____

_____

_____

_____

_____

_____

_____

_____

_____

_____

_____

_____

Love What You Do

Success is something we all want
within our lives each day.
Some will know how to achieve it
while others go astray.

What can we do to capture
the ideas that will grow?
What channels do we follow
to show others what we know?

We let our great minds wander,
soon soaring to heights above;
but, what can we do to succeed
in doing things we love?

Set goals we can accomplish
and feel good with things we do.
If we love what we are doing
our worries will be few.

If we succeed with small steps,
and use them to build our way,
we will soon be feeling better
about each passing day.

We will gradually climb the ladder
towards a higher place.
We will soon feel the radiance
of success upon our face.

Remember in our journey
as we climb up from the ground,
do what we love each day we live
until success is found.

Look into your heart. What do you truly want in your life? Are you doing what you love? What steps can you take towards where you want to be and what you want to do?

Who can help you work towards doing what you love?

_____

_____

_____

_____

_____

_____

_____

_____

_____

_____

_____

_____

_____

_____

_____

_____

Life

A seed is planted and I begin to form,
it will be nine months now until I am born.
The warmth will continue to envelop me
until the time arrives for me to be free.

Upon the day I have chosen to arrive
I won't take any chances, as I need to survive.
The lights are so bright as I exit the womb
I'll give a big stretch, as I'll finally have room.

Room to experience all things that are new.
A quick look around, there are things to do.
I must learn to talk, that's a sure thing,
A sigh or a coo, attention it will bring.

Soon I shall try some words that are fun,
"Momma" or "Dadda", bring them on the run.
When they arrive at my side, I pop a big smile
I never have to wait more than a short while.

I grow some more with each passing day,
hoping that there will be time for some play.
A story is read to me, a song is now sung,
the words I repeat with the tip of my tongue.

The next thing for me is to crawl all around,
looking for toys and other treasures found.
But, crawlin's too slow for my speedy pace,
so up on my feet, I am ready to race.

It's hard to believe that one year has now passed,
I hope that fun playtimes always will last.
I see a big cake now coming my way,
"Happy Birthday" it says on this special day.

Over the next few years I learn how to share,
to play with my friends and show that I care.
I play with my toys, some old and some new.
My grandparents see me, "Oh my, how you grew!"

I'm getting bigger and bigger they say.
I want new adventures with each passing day.
My pets I take care of, it is something I do,
as they love me no matter the things that I do.

After this summer, to school I will go,
my numbers and letters, soon I will know.
And after a while I'll be able to read.
Its important you know, it's a thing that you need.

As the years fly right by one, two, three, and four,
I want to continue, I want to learn more.
Math is now simple, I calculate with ease,
I can solve most problems as quick as I please.

They say that it's tougher the older you get,
but I'm still a learnin'; I'm not finished yet.
Social has taught me many cultural things,
while Science has informed me of what nature brings.

The next stage in my life, they call me a 'teen',
the trouble that follows has yet to be seen.
There are ups and downs as emotions flare,
I can get through this now I have people who care.

The more that I learn now, that I can apply,
will help me later in life, one cannot deny.
Of debits and credits and budgets just right,
plus all of the skills I have learned when I write.

I put all of the skills that I know to good use
in each subject I tackle, my brain I turn loose.
I want to absorb everything, all that I can,
I know I will use it; it's in the great plan.

So as the years passed, I awaited this day,
to complete my high school and then move away.
To get out on my own and try out all I learned,
a few jobs available, maybe one which I yearned.

Through all of the people I met as I grew
there would be someone special for me that I knew.
That one individual with whom to share life
so that we together would be husband and wife.

Once we were ready to be more than two,
a seed would be planted by a love that is true.
A new life would begin with love all around,
the growth, trials and learning were again to be found.

Time passes quickly as years fly right by,
children grow up and we await their good-bye.
The nest is then empty; we find new things to do
and before we knew it, the grandchildren grew.

We know that our lives are what we choose.
We try to be winners, but sometimes we lose.
As all good things we know must come to an end,
at sometime we must say, "Goodbye my dear friends!"

Life is a mirror of everything we do and say. We need to reflect upon events in our lives to appreciate where we are. This week think of one thing you would like to do before it is your time to say goodbye. Make a plan of how you will accomplish this final dream.

_____

_____

_____

_____

_____

_____

_____

_____

_____

_____

_____

_____

_____

_____

_____

_____

_____